Dream To Reality

How to Train Your Mind to Achieve Your Goals

D. GROSSART
J. KATTENBERG

© 2013 REALITY PRODUCTIONS LTD.

ALL RIGHTS RESERVED. NO PART OF THIS WORK MAY BE REPRODUCED OR STORED IN AN INFORMATIONAL RETRIEVAL SYSTEM, WITHOUT THE EXPRESS PERMISSION OF THE PUBLISHER IN WRITING.

CONTACT@REALITYPRODUCTIONS.CO.UK

ISBN: 978-0-9927480-0-5

"Watch your thoughts; they become words.
Watch your words; they become actions.
Watch your actions; they become habits.
Watch your habits; they become character.
Watch your character; it becomes your destiny."

Lao-Tzu

(Chinese Philosopher, 6th Century)

CONTENTS

PREFACE	1
INTRODUCTION	3
GUIDANCE NOTES	7
1. THE IMMENSE POTENTIAL IN YOU	13
2. THE POWER OF YOUR OWN MIND	23
3. YOUR BIG DREAM – THE PROCESS OF GOAL CREATION	33
4. DAILY HABITS FOR SUCCESS	41
5. WHAT'S YOUR BIG WHY?	55
6. YOUR PERSONAL 5 A'S	63
7. NURTURING YOUR BODY AND LIVING WELL	75
SUMMARY	79

Author's Preface:

When we began this project, we didn't know quite how it would come to fruition; we just knew that somehow we'd find a way to make it happen. We want to inspire as many people as possible to achieve more for themselves, contribute to others, dream bigger and understand that whatever difficulties they face, there is *always* a way to overcome them in some way, while enjoying life in the process.

Our family mantra is 'Anything Is Possible' and this project truly tested our own belief and resourcefulness. We're so proud to have achieved what we have, and we aim to help thousands of people gain new skills and build self-belief while raising funds to make a lasting difference to the lives of many people.

Everyone has challenges, dreams and mountains to climb...but when you understand that there is a proven process to building confidence and self-belief for personal achievement that can be applied by anyone, in any circumstances, at any age in life, you have the keys to unlock your true potential.

Thanks to all of our supporters, sponsors, family and friends who have helped us to make our own dream come true and make our own difference in the world. We can't thank you enough and send all our love and gratitude.

Dawn Grossart & Jonathan Kattenberg

Introduction:

Choose your dream, and dream BIG. If you could have anything in life – and enjoy the most incredible journey, what would it look like? This book is written to show you that you CAN achieve *anything* when you know how. Let no one deter you. Be committed to yourself and your chosen goals until you have felt the swelling pride of achievement in yourself.

There are some things that adults find difficult to explain to younger people, the truths and realisations that come with age and experience. Often things can seem perhaps a little unreal or "far-fetched to explain or understand.

Many adults have to work hard later in life to undo bad habits that prevent success. We want to give you the tools to prevent bad habits becoming established, so YOU have a head start in life.

We believe that what's written here should be accessible to anyone and everyone to help them make the best of themselves and to enjoy an amazing life – because everyone should have the opportunity to experience a fulfilling life and become the best person they can possibly be. This is the introduction to a way of thinking which has been proven time and time again to be the source of fulfilment in life.

It's easy to be influenced by negative comments and beliefs, but when you keep a positive focus, you can override anything to achieve GREAT things.

This book can help you develop greater self-confidence and to create the life you really want using techniques and practices that many people don't discover until much later in life - if ever. If you choose to read, embrace and practice its contents, you'll create advantages for yourself in life. You're about to receive an insight into a world of achievement which is often left to chance discovery and is not yet taught as a matter of course.

It works for anyone. You do however have to be inspired to follow the process and be committed – that's one of the greatest challenges of all. As many have said before us, "It's simple, but it's not easy."

You'll discover that what you actually *think*

determines your experience of life and **that you can *fundamentally control this*** to be whoever you want to be and achieve what you really want.

This is a simple but incredibly powerful truth. Grasp the full meaning and your potential is endless.

If followed closely, this book will help you learn to control your own thoughts and create a resilient, positive mind-set so that you can stay focussed to achieve whatever it is that your heart desires, whatever inspires you.

Knowing what you *really* want for yourself in life gives you a great advantage. Many people don't know what they want. Most don't really believe that they can achieve it, so they limit themselves and their achievement. According to success author and speaker Brian Tracy, only 3 people in 100 have clearly identified written goals expressing specifically what they want to achieve in life. When you start thinking and *feeling* what you'd like your life to be like and believing it can happen, Listen to your intuition, let it guide you and see where it takes you…

Don't be put off by the magnitude of your ultimate dreams and goals. Just start by setting smaller ones first and build up from there, step by step. Allow for realism, understand there may be some failure along the way, but trust yourself and the process you are about to discover.

Enjoy your journey, have fun, be strong and go out and achieve whatever it is that you want in life.

Finally, don't imagine for a moment that you have to do this all by yourself. Although you'll be exploring *your own* personal goals, you'll need help from others in some way to achieve them. Never be afraid to ask trusted, positive friends to help you.

Commit right now to your own success in life and to achieving the very best that you possibly can.

We are here to support you too.

You can reach us on
contact@realityproductions.co.uk

Guidance Notes:

These notes are written to help support your understanding and use of this book.

People of all ages can benefit from this information. However, if you're under 15 you might want to work with a supportive adult or friend who can help if you need it.

If there are words or ideas you don't understand, please look them up and discover new knowledge for yourself.

We can't stress enough how it takes time and commitment to make changes and achieve great things – however, it CAN be done – by ANYONE, at ANY TIME and you're no different!

Rather than put lots of case studies in this book, we want you to make this book ***your own case study*** to show that anything is possible when you know what you want and believe you can do it. Results will depend on your dedication to your improvement.

This book is a taster of a wide range of reading

and resources about the power of a positive and focussed mind-set. If you find it interesting, please refer to the Appendix for further reading.

Buy yourself a quality notebook to keep with you that will become your journal to capture thoughts, ideas and complete the written exercises as you read through the book.

"Set your sights high, the higher the better. Expect the most wonderful things to happen, not in the future but right now. Realize that nothing is too good. Allow absolutely nothing to hamper you or hold you up in any way."

Eileen Caddy MBE (1917-2006)

Spiritual Teacher

EXERCISE:

Write a list of goals – things you'd like to achieve, things you'd love to have or things you'd like to change.

As you read through this book, refer back to this page and use it as the starting point to achieving great things for yourself.

DREAM TO REALITY

Chapter 1

THE IMMENSE POTENTIAL IN YOU

It's a fact that your power is truly infinite. *No one knows the limits of human potential* – boundaries have never been established. Every miraculous invention, structure, organisation and achievement began as an idea which someone then developed and made a reality. Your imagination is a uniquely powerful tool that is capable of great things when you learn how to apply it. The quality of your life depends on it.

The only boundaries that exist are the ones that you create in your own mind. So, let your imagination be your best friend, your strongest ally and your route to success, happiness and freedom.

Something which you need to be very clear about is that most people who fail to live how they'd really like to, or don't achieve their full potential, do so because they are thrown off course by the negativity of others, or by challenges and obstacles which seem too difficult to overcome.

Positivity is contagious – and so is the energy which goes with it. Think of someone you know who is always upbeat, positive and full of encouragement. Now think of someone who is often negative, complains or sees the worst – how do they make you feel? What are YOU like with others, such as your friends and family?

We all bring energy to situations based on our thoughts and feelings. We all have the power to determine whether that energy will be positive or negative, generous and enthusiastic or selfish and moody. When you decide that you will be positive and that you will achieve what you want, you will start to see how things happen for the better!

Is your glass half full or half empty? What is your attitude and perspective on life generally? Having a "glass half-full" outlook on life, means that you always look at situations in a positive way and this is proven to create better results in whatever you do.

When you want to achieve something for yourself in life, YOU have to create and sustain the driving force until you have got to where you want to be. When you do something like learning to swim or drive a car, YOU have to make the effort – no else can do it for you. The same is true for everything you will ever achieve.

Surrounding yourself with the right people who genuinely support you is one of the best decisions you can ever make. Be strong and don't fall victim to peer pressure, cherish your independence and your own ambitions. Celebrate that you are unique. Reject the negative, in whatever form you find it. One of the greatest lessons you can learn is that the people around you can be the greatest help or the greatest hindrance, blocking your progress or even causing you to quit by being negative, telling you that something's not possible. When this happens, walk away and think positively. You'll do better next time.

Our modern media driven society *can be* a really negative influence for people wanting to make positive change in their life. It's so important to focus on positive thoughts and things to help you be successful. The media makes big stories from disaster and economic hardship, and that brings bad news and negativity into your living room almost every day. Whilst we shouldn't ignore what goes on around us, you have to ask the question, "Does this contribute to the creation of fear and a general lack of confidence in some individuals, families, communities, even nations?"

For example, if everything you hear is negative it makes it harder to stay positive, which is why you must be able to train your mind to remain confident and positive.

Today's social media plays a major part in supporting positivity or being a detrimental negative influence. Confidence, self-believe and personal results can all be affected by what you read and what your "friends" say.

Your Moral Code:

What is your moral code? I.e. being kind and not judging others until you know the full facts? Are you totally honest to yourself and your friends and family?

You'll discover in life that often those who achieve the most have a solid moral code by which they live.

Remember, we're talking here about a process based on self-belief. Positivity works for everyone and ANYONE – you just have to be true to the process and your own heart.

EXERCISE:

What is YOUR moral code? Can you list the values and the actions that represent you being a good person?

"Always do what is right. It will gratify half of mankind and astound the other."

Mark Twain (1835-1910)
American Author

Feeling good inside by being honest with yourself and others helps you to keep a very positive outlook.

Choosing to be with people who make you FEEL good, happy and enthusiastic is the best way to create positive energy. Choose to reject the negative thoughts and messages of our modern media-driven world. We will show you in later chapters how to defend your mind from negative thoughts and develop practical ways to increase positive thinking.

Engaging in gossip, mistreating or talking cruelly of others is detrimental. If you decide to make kindness and positivity your goal every day, you will start to FEEL better about yourself and your world. When this starts to happen, your experience of life starts to change. Is this hard to believe? Try it. Genuinely live good values and kindness as the theme to your life and more kindness and goodness will come back to you. The saying, "What goes around, come around" means that whatever you do, and however you behave, is the measure of what you will receive in return.

Adopting "An attitude of gratitude" means that you start to look for all of the things and people in your world that you're grateful for – this will help you to focus on all of the positive things that you have in life. Like attracts like, so you will find that the more you are grateful for what you have, the more you attract more good into your world.

It doesn't cost anything to be nice, but it goes a VERY long way...

Chapter 2

THE POWER OF YOUR MIND

We are all capable of individual greatness. Over the last century much has been written about human power and potential which has been researched and proven to be true. It's scientifically understood that you have a CONSCIOUS mind and a SUB-CONSCIOUS mind. Each performs a distinct and very different role in your experience of life. One great truth is that you must guard your sub-conscious mind from negative thoughts and fill it with all the focussed positivity possible.

Here's an example to explain the conscious and sub-conscious mind. Remember the first time you learned to ride a bike, or swim? You had to think hard about the movements you were making to stay balanced or afloat, but with practice and experience it became second nature and the movements became "natural" and you did them *without thinking*? The activity moved from consciously "thinking" to effortlessly "doing" automatically.

So much of what you do is sub-conscious, and your very powerful mind can support great success or hinder your progress by accepting messages or developing beliefs that hold you back.

Conscious Mind:

Your conscious mind gathers and processes information from the world around you, creating your reality based on what you see and from experiences and messages that enter your brain through the senses – sight, sound, touch, smell and taste. Gathering information from your environment and your experiences, your conscious mind feeds information into your sub-conscious. This then forms beliefs and expectations. However right or wrong, these beliefs and expectations shape your character, your personality and your behaviour – creating your experience of life.

Sub-conscious mind

Your sub-conscious mind is the major part of your programming which controls behaviours and beliefs, which in turn controls your actions. When you know how to control and master *it*, you have a very real advantage indeed.

Your sub-conscious mind acts automatically, "without thinking". It is *totally* programmable because it receives information from your conscious mind – it's like your own inner computer – and you must learn how to put the best information in, which will serve you in life, and ensure that any damaging, unhelpful and harmful thoughts are kept at bay – because these will block your path to achieving your goals and possibly even destroy your dreams.

When you recognise unhelpful thoughts and beliefs coming to mind, you can stop this by literally changing the programme – altering your thinking.

For example, take a negative thought such as "I can't do this" and changing it for a positive belief "I CAN do it and I WILL". It takes practice but it *does* work. It sounds simple, but it's not easy, you need to practice and be committed to yourself.

What this book helps you to do is programme yourself with new habits, thoughts and beliefs to improve your experience of life. Think bigger, feel stronger and believe that YOU ABSOLUTELY CAN.

Follow the step-by-step guide and over time you'll begin to see and feel a difference in yourself. It takes at least 30 days of consecutive practice to start to feel improvements and 90 days to begin to really shift a gear.

EXERCISE:

Follow each step precisely and in time, you will begin to see positive changes.

1. Fix in your mind a goal you would like to achieve. Be as specific as you can.
2. Decide what you are prepared to do or give to achieve this – for example a daily commitment to do something that will take you towards your goal.
3. Establish a definite date that you intend to have achieved your goal.
4. Create a definite plan of how you will move towards your desired goal and begin straight away.
5. Write on a piece of paper a clear, concise statement of the goal you intend to achieve in, the time scale to achieve it and what you will do, or give, to achieve it.
6. Read your written statement aloud, twice daily once at night before bed and once in the morning when you get up. As you read it, SEE yourself achieving your goal in your mind.

Write your Goal Statement here, in the present tense – as though you have already achieved:

By (date)

I'm so happy and grateful now that I have

Put this statement somewhere where you can see it often, every day – such as next to your bed or on your mobile phone.

This is the basis of mind training that has created some of the most successful people in history, such as former American President Abraham Lincoln, and is becoming more and more accepted and understood today. We all have the ability to change and overcome any circumstances. It is how we think and train our minds that determines where we go and what we achieve in life. If you can understand this, you have huge potential. You can actually CHOOSE what you think and believe.

SO, decide to start. Know that it's a long-distance race. Don't expect overnight results of quick fixes. Patience and commitment to yourself is key. If you can keep yourself focussed on this task you will soon start to feel positive differences in yourself. If you miss a day, start again, counting this day as day 1 until you have achieved 30 consecutive days...then make it 90 days....this is where change really starts to happen. Decide that the price you have to pay in the commitment of time, focus and effort is worth it to get to where you really want to be.

If you can believe it, you can achieve it.

When you mentally create an image in your mind of something you want to achieve, you have put yourself on the first rung of the ladder to reach it.

The more you focus your mental energy on your ambition, and the more you become emotionally involved with the feelings of it, the greater your desire will become and you will start to feel yourself want it even more. Try it. Get emotionally involved with *feeling good* about the achievement of your dream and you will start to feel increased strength of motivation with the frequency of repetition. Here, you are building a strong foundation to move towards creating a new reality for yourself over time.

When we know that 'feeling good' about ourselves is important for achievement, then the way we behave towards others becomes a vital consideration! When you choose to be your best self, kind, honest and with a clear conscience then you put yourself in the best possible place for progress. Winners are good, kind, honest focussed people who don't make enemies nor cause ill-feeling for others.

Decide to be the best, kindest person that you can be. Start with a commitment to be and to do your very best in everything. This is the basis of achievement, success and self-fulfilment, from where you can experience the joy and satisfaction of living at your very best, highest level.

Be totally honest with yourself and explore how and where you can make improvements to be a better person.

Coming up later in the book is another practical

framework to help you move towards achieving the goals you choose for yourself and set you on the path to training your mind for your individual success.

It's important to say here that while we're exploring ways to achieve success, and for you to be your best self, you must recognise that not every action you choose to take will be successful. Failure in life DOES happen. What's important is how you choose to handle failure. Sometimes failures are the basis of our most significant learning in life.

Learn to never be a quitter.

According to Napoleon Hill, leading authority on the human success formula, it is just when you think you have tried everything possible to achieve your goal that the very important opportunity to achieve it arises.

Thomas Edison, inventor of the incandescent light bulb, famously carried out over 10,000 experiments before finally discovering the answer in 1879.

"Whether you think that you can, or that you can't, you are usually right."

Henry Ford (1863-1947)

Founder of Motor Motors

Chapter 3

THE IMPORTANCE OF YOUR VISION AND THE PROCESS OF GOAL CREATION

If you have no goals in life, then how can you do anything other than drift aimlessly, with only moderate results? Sadly, this is how many people go through life. We're hoping that this book will lead you to explore more deeply how to unlock your true potential – because undoubtedly, it's greater than you think!

Ask yourself what your own personal definition of success is – this will help you set goals for yourself.

EVERYONE has the potential to succeed at ANYTHING they choose to commit themselves to. You just have to believe you can do it. Your personal happiness, fulfilment and satisfaction will come from your own efforts in whatever it is that you love to do or WANT to achieve.

Entrepreneurial guru Richard Branson believes

that goal setting from an early age is the key to a successful life of significant achievement.

Decide to be different from everyone else. Create a vision in your mind of yourself living a life you love, spending time doing things that you love to do, with people you enjoy being with. How fantastic would that be? Well, know this. It's possible. YOU have the power to create it.

When you commit yourself to a goal and focus on it every day, it becomes upper-most in your conscious mind. Your sub-conscious tunes into it, creating ideas and thoughts to help you. Actively creating ideas and solutions "on purpose" is a practice that can be nurtured by having relaxing quiet time alone, with no interruptions and allowing your thoughts to flow. Ask yourself "how do I do…?" or "what's the best way for me to…" and see what flows into your mind.

Although you might think that your dream or vision is beyond your reach, take the first step and have faith that you'll be able to achieve it. Try it with sincerity and you will find things start to happen.

When Napoleon Hill wrote the famous book Think and Grow Rich in the 1930's he spent over 20 years interviewing 500 of America's most successful people. He discovered that there was a common thread to all of those success stories and that boils down to the following essentials:

- A clearly stated vision or purpose
- A daily habit to keep you focussed and positive – in belief and faith of ultimate success
- A commitment to be your very best, persistently maintain belief, positive thoughts and take action
- An emotional connection to your purpose – a feel good sensation which supports your desire to achieve.
- A supportive group of people who can help you achieve your vision and a mind closed to negativity

Belief

People may say to you "believe in yourself" or "have faith" but they rarely explain how you manage to do this. You now know that the subconscious mind can be programmed like your own personal computer, you can literally choose what you want to think and believe. That might sound far-fetched – but try it and you will eventually prove it to yourself.

It is the process of "self-influencing" through repetition that creates results. Right thoughts supported by right actions.

For example, if you want to build self-confidence, create a statement such as "I am confident when I meet new people" and re-write it many times every day and *say it out loud with feeling.*

Visualise yourself in a situation, acting confidently, head held high, being the perfectly confident person you want to be. If you have been there in your mind, you can get there in your body. This process of visualisation has been described by many people who have discovered this process for themselves, such as athletes and performers.

They say that *expectation* is the mysterious ingredient. It seems that when you expect a particular outcome, this is often what turns out to be true – so expect good things to happen!

Your results will be individual. Yours and yours alone. So ask yourself, "What is it that I want to do or achieve the most?"

You must have a strong and burning ambition and personal drive to succeed! If you want to build a *stronger* drive to succeed, use your mental strength and powers to help you. Keep focussing on your vision and feeling positive inside, and keep repeating the words and studying the images that you associate with that feeling.

If you focus on it and repeat it out loud twice a day for 15 minutes for 90 consecutive days you will definitely feel very differently at the end!

Although the exercise in itself if simple, much effort is needed to maintain it, so be patient and persistent. Decide for yourself that you want to have a fantastic, successful life - and believe that you will get there eventually, wherever you are right now.

Pursue your goal with commitment until you've enjoyed the success of achieving it. Have fun in the process – remember that whatever your circumstances or challenges, there IS a positive way forward.

India's Affirmation:

15 year old India had very bad eczema on her face when she started senior school at 11. It was so bad she had to go to hospital 3 times a week for light therapy. Her Dad kept reminding her to look at herself in the mirror every morning, wink at herself and say "Hey Good Looking!" This really helped her self-confidence and even now, she still looks in the mirror and says "Hey Good Looking!" every morning and feels great for the rest of the day. Her skin may feel like the enemy at times, but she *feels* and *knows* that she is beautiful person.

Why not try creating a helpful affirmation for yourself, which generates a very positive feeling in you and sets up your intention to feel good every day?

E.g. I am a confident, good person and I am successful.

*"Here in my heart,
my happiness, my house.*

*Here inside the lighted window is
my love, my hope, my life.*

*Peace is my companion on the
pathway winding to the threshold.*

*Inside this portal dwells new strength
in the security, serenity, and radiance
of those I love above life itself.*

*Here two will build new dreams-dreams
that tomorrow will come true.*

*The world over, these are the
thoughts at eventide when footsteps
turn ever homeward.*

*In the haven of the hearthside is
rest and peace and comfort."*

Abraham Lincoln (1809-1865)

US President

Chapter 4

DAILY HABITS FOR SUCCESS

The challenge each of us faces, in varying degrees is developing confidence in who we are, what we can do and the self-belief that we can actually do it. For some people confidence comes easily, naturally – but for others, it has to be a conscious choice to develop it, pushing beyond comfort zones to grow and improve.

Your Personal Confidence Tool Kit

We've explained earlier that it's possible to programme your own thoughts and to choose your mood, levels of energy and enthusiasm through what you're thinking. It's also possible to build self-confidence through what you think and tell yourself in your mind.

You can eventually start to change the way you behave and think – becoming the person you want to be, possessing the traits you want to possess through your own conscious choice. You can also begin to change the circumstances in which you live and your levels of enjoyment in life.

We've introduced earlier that "Affirmations" are statements or mind-tools that you can use to improve and enhance your mind-set and increase your levels of self-belief and confidence. They are 'self programming' messages to help build your self-belief and mental strength.

Imagine that you're preparing for a big event, a show or performance – you're doing well, but feeling nervous and anxious about your performance on the big day. Here's something that will help you through and achieve the outcome you desire:

1. It helps to close your eyes. Imagine yourself in the situation, seeing in your mind's eye the perfect result that you dream of. Make a detailed picture in your mind of the situation, place or event and make it ***feel real. Remember that your subconscious accepts as real the thoughts and images that you place there. Using your conscious mind to focus your thoughts in this way is one of the most beneficial uses of your imagination and can be genuinely life changing.***
2. *Feel* the positive emotions inside you. As part of the visualisation journey, notice how you feel inside. Imagining situations that you like or enjoy creates feelings of happiness and positivity. The more positive you feel about an outcome or a situation, the greater the chance of success. You will feel more motivated and committed to its

achievement. Repeat the words that will help you achieve – i.e. "I am confident" or "I have achieved x" or "I am a winner."

A quiet mind is a more creative, fertile mind. High achievers will all tell you that they create time and space to relax and to use their imaginations in a productive way. Generating ideas and thoughts that bring solutions and help find answers to problems is harder to find when your mind is busy and over loaded.

Relaxation techniques, such as meditation are the inner secret of many people who've achieved their dreams and created the life they imagined for themselves. We've already mentioned that a fertile imagination is important – so it's helpful to understand that creativity flows to the relaxed mind. Focus on what it is you are trying to achieve and allow your mind to inspire you.

You might find that sitting in a quiet place by yourself for a few minutes each day, closing your eyes and taking long, slow, deep breaths while thinking about your goal or ambition, you will make positive associations and connections in your mind. Ideas may come that will help feel more focussed and inspired. Solutions to problems or creative ideas may arise.

Using both the written word and visual imagery is an important and fun way to support your creativity and bring your dreams to life. Enjoy creating the beginnings of the life you choose for yourself and allow your sub-conscious mind to find the best ways to help you achieve it over time.

"Words create images, images create feelings and feelings create actions" says Bob Proctor, world authority on human achievement.

When we write, we inspire our own imagination and feed our thoughts with details which help us. Try this, make it fun. The more you enjoy it and feel good about it, the higher your energy will be and your level of positivity. Writing every day and finding pictures to represent what you want to achieve are part of a magical process of mental creativity. Your sub-conscious mind can be your best friend or your worst enemy. At times, all of us face challenges to tame negativity and focus on the positive possibilities. Taming your unhelpful thoughts and just being aware that you can choose to replace them with good ones is what we want to help you do. Be aware of the thoughts that hinder you and use this process every day to develop your positive thoughts, energy, and ability to focus on achieving your goal or ambition.

Here's a task to complete:

List 30 goals that you'd like to achieve – they can be anything at all. You MUST have 30! Not 25 or 28, there is a reason for this.

When you have a list of 30, go through the list and decide which 10 are the most important to you. Rank these all as "A" goals, and then do the same again with the next 10, ranking them as "B" goals, the remaining 10 as "C" goals. The C Goals are where you start and they form your important early stepping stones to achieving your goals and building the life you want.

My Goals:

Goal	A	B	C
1			
2			
3			
4			
5			
6			
7			
8			
9			
10			
11			

Goal	A	B	C
12			
13			
14			
15			
16			
17			
18			
19			
20			
21			
22			
23			
24			
25			
26			
27			
28			
29			
30			

List All Your A, B, and C Goals here so you can see them clearly

A Goals
1
2
3
4
5
6
7
8
9
10
B Goals
1
2
3
4
5
6
7
8

9	
10	
C Goals	
1	
2	
3	
4	
5	
6	
7	
8	
9	
10	

Your C Goals will be those that are less stretching than your A and B Goals, so start with aiming to achieve these first and you will get into the habit of working with setting and achieving goals.

Your Treasure Map

Make your goals real with pictures.

Using the internet, magazines, photographs or any source that inspires you, select images that you love to look at that represent your goals. Create a "Treasure Map" of things you'd choose to have in your life. As described previously, make some quiet time, perhaps 10-15 minutes every day to think about yourself being, having or doing the things you've chosen for yourself. Feel the positive feelings rise in you as your mind creates the positive connection with your images. This is a proven strategy that almost all goal achievers use in some way. Emotion is the key.

Make sure you include images that represent you as a confident successful person with a fit, healthy body.

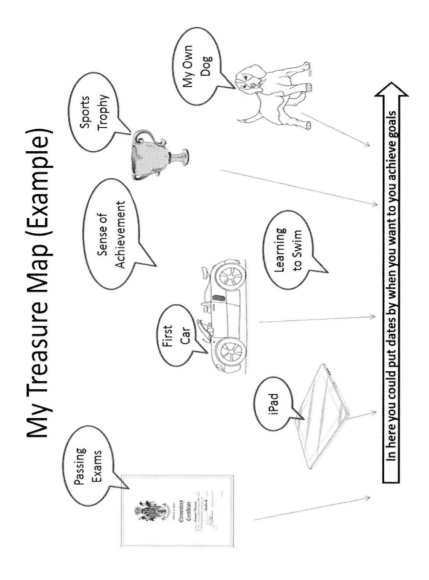

Regular, persistent repetition of the process keeps your mind in the right zone and your positivity and enthusiasm in the best possible place for achievement. Use your Treasure Map and your written statement together to really fire up your feelings about your goals. Create the amazing positive emotions that will help to drive you on to be the very best version of you possible.

When you have a strong emotional connection with your goals and you frequently create "feel good" energy, you are very firmly on the right track and moving in the right direction.

Whilst it might sound an odd way to describe becoming your best self, we'll talk about "raising your frequency". Everything that exists on the earth has a frequency at which it vibrates or resonates, that's a proven fact of scientific physics. Human bodies also have an energetic frequency. When we understand this, we can change it. When we focus our minds on the things that make us feel good, the more we attract the positive energies that will help us. We naturally find people and circumstances that are "in tune" with us and our goals.

Here's an example to demonstrate the point. Think of a person who is bounding with joy and enthusiasm – they are often great to be around and they tend to attract people who are on the same wavelength as themselves. Someone who is negative and moans also emits energy, but this energy is negative and much less attractive to most people.

We attract more of what we are, much as a magnet attracts to itself. So the more we improve ourselves and raise our frequency, the more we attract people who can help us improve even more.

Positive Emotions:

Excitement   *Enthusiasm*

Joy   *Happiness*

Caring   *Giving*

Supporting   *Celebrating*

Negative Emotions:

Criticism   *Fear*

Anxiety   *Negativity*

Gossiping   *Procrastination*

Add to this list any positive or negative emotions that you need to be aware of and watch for in yourself.

If you can do your very best to reject negative ways and emotions, and decide to always act from a place of love and consideration for yourself and others, your experience of life will change and you will enjoy increased support of others and improved progress as a result.

"We can complain because rose bushes have thorns, or rejoice because thorn bushes have roses."

Abraham Lincoln

Chapter 5

WHAT'S YOUR BIG 'WHY?'

Ask yourself, "Why" are you setting out to achieve your particular goals and ambitions? Is it for your personal satisfaction or to do something to help others?

There's no right or wrong answer – and it is totally personal to you, but the clearer you are about what motivates you, the easier it will be for you to identify the thoughts, feelings or images that connect your goals to your actions.

Use the space below to write down your reasons why you want to achieve your goal.

....

....

....

....

....

....

The reason we've asked you to identify *the reason* for achieving your goal is that when your desire and motivation is strong, you won't allow anything or anyone to deter you. Keep your desire and motivation strong by using your imagination as we described earlier to fuel positive feelings of achievement.

The Olympic athlete will tell you that they visualise seeing themselves passing the winning post and standing on the winner's podium, receiving their medal. They visualise and "feel" it with such intensity – they want it so badly that they are prepared to do whatever it takes to achieve it – that can often be many, many years, day in, day out of hard work, gruelling commitment and sometimes heartache. They want it badly enough to make sacrifices, and when the achievement finally comes it is the best feeling imaginable!

For some people, self-fulfilment is the overwhelming motivator, whereas others are motivated by helping others and making a bigger difference to their family, community or society as a whole. It is said that often, to be motivated by doing good and making a difference for others is far more powerful than anything else.

Ask yourself – what's your motivation? How strong is it? What will keep you fired up and on track when the going gets tough?

The Power of Fulfilment-Focus

We're now going to look at two sides of the situation. If you have a dream, an ambition and a desire to be, do or have something in your life – ask yourself these two questions and see which one *feels* the best to you.

1. "What will I feel like if I never have it, do it or achieve it?"

Write your thoughts here: (or write in your journal)

_____

_____

_____

_____

_____

_____

_____

_____

You'll possibly answer with words like frustrated, disappointed, unhappy or unfulfilled. Perhaps empty, or regret for not applying yourself to try and achieve?

Now this:

2) "What will I feel like if have it, do it and achieve it?

Using your imagination and the power of your creative mind to visualise, close your eyes and mentally step into the situation you want to happen. Can you create a new feeling with the power of your thoughts? If so, you'll possibly describe the feelings as satisfying, fulfilling, truly happy within, exciting etc. Maybe relief, accomplished, awesome, warm, humble, grateful.

Write your thoughts here: (or write in your journal)

When you identify the positive thoughts and feelings that make you feel good about your goal keep re-visiting them often every day – ideally in the morning when you get up and in the evening before you go to bed, as well as throughout the day. What you're doing is fuelling your sub-conscious mind and telling it every day that this is what you want to be doing and how you want to be living. Your sub-conscious ALWAYS works with what you give it and helps bring about the results of what you focus on. So make it positive and believe you can achieve it.

The challenge that each and every one of us has, is to ensure that the positive thoughts and images outweigh the negative. Remember, when a negative thought pops into your head, recognise it, then consciously over-ride it with a positive one. Visualise a positive situation, create a positive feeling and thought. **This is your own personal success powerhouse.**

When we can tune into that voice in our mind and be conscious of what it's telling us, we have the power to change and manage things for the greater good of ourselves and for the good of others. EVERYTHING ultimately depends on the quality and consistency of your self-talk – that inner voice within.

Having a purpose, moving gradually towards it and ultimately achieving it creates fulfilment. It gives us a reason to live and to get out of bed every day. It removes frustration, doubt and makes the difference to our experience of life.

If you haven't already got a life-vision for yourself, decide to spend some fun time creating that mental image of you in a life you would love to be living and commit your energies to make it become real. You really can do anything when you believe it.

Commit your vision to writing and pictures, then begin to regularly visualise yourself living that life.

"Leap and the Net will appear"
John Burroughs
(April 3, 1837 – March 29, 1921)

John Burroughs was an American naturalist and essayist important in the evolution of the U.S. conservation movement.

Chapter 6

YOUR PERSONAL 5 A'S

In this chapter, we introduce a framework for you to memorize and work with. Your starting point is wherever you are now in life – whatever age or circumstances – you can use this to help you identify the things you can do to change your circumstances or results.

Success Formula

Acknowledge: It's important to understand where you're at right now in relation to achieving your challenge or goal. What are your obstacles and what is working in your favour?

For example, a climber planning to summit a challenging mountain must appreciate and acknowledge a wide variety of factors, such as physical fitness and strength, technical ability, resources such as finance, equipment, time and key areas of support. You must also undergo a similar process of evaluating your situation and recognising what is needed to fulfil your goal.

Once you have a full appreciation of your current situation, you can map out the route and gather your resources to make forward progress.

Acknowledge Exercise: Write down your goal in detail and then list the areas that you need to manage or change.

Hints: Do you have to learn a new skill or improve an existing ability? Do you need to save an amount of money to buy an essential piece of equipment? Do you need to establish a team of colleagues? Ask yourself "What is the best solution to this challenge and see what answers come to you".

Accept: You may have to face limitations, frustrations or fears. Recognising and accepting things that we cannot change can be a challenging thing to do. However when we learn to accept things that we cannot change, we free ourselves from the mental conflict which can arise from constant frustration of focussing on something beyond our control.

Write down each of the limitations, frustrations or fears that you recognise could prevent you from making changes and achieving your goals or dreams. The purpose of this exercise is to identify what support you might need to help you achieve your goals and to recognise the practical steps, pros and cons and immediate challenges you need to overcome. Whilst we encourage ambition and ultimately highly stretching goals, there are steps to be taken, one at a time and recognising the areas that are more challenging will help you to work upon the areas that you *can influence* more actively first.

Accept Exercise:

Agree: Make a deal with yourself that you are worthy of more than you have and are right now. That you're worthy of achieving your greatest potential and decide that you will do what it takes to get where you want to get to.

Set realistic timescales. The next exercise will help you make the commitment to yourself. What you can then do is create a life-map or vision board to chart your progress. At this stage, it is as important as any other section to write things down. Using this book (or your journal) you can list the bullet points on this page of the timescales of the activities you need to do or the resources you need to gather.

Accept Exercise:

Act Now: When you have committed yourself to pursuing and achieving a specific objective, practice your mental exercises every day! However, without action, nothing can change physically. You have to go out and do things, meet people who can help, put things in place, travel and just actually start **_DOING_** things. You need a plan of actions that will get you started – even though you might not actually know at this stage how you'll achieve every step. Opportunities arise along the way which you could never have imagined – so keep an open mind and be vigilant for the people and circumstances that can help you.

Recognise what your priorities are and don't be distracted by other things that don't positively contribute to your achievement. Commit to do something *every day* which takes you closer towards your goal.

To prevent distraction from other things or people, spend time to identify the people, distractions or negative influences that could have an impact on your progress. Decide then to be strong in the face of any negativity or distraction when it arises.

Act Now Exercise:

Achieve:

When you have the right mental attitude and a plan to get started, everything that has been outlined in previous pages will help you move towards achievement. You might decide to give yourself small milestones to aim for and celebrate small wins along the way. The great thing is you will be on your journey to achieving your goals, because you will be doing something every day to help you get to your destination, whilst nurturing and developing a mental attitude for greatness in your own way.

Rewarding others is an absolute must too, especially where key individuals have made a significant difference to help you. This does not have to be a costly exercise – it could be a simple thank you card, but it's the thought that counts and actually making the gesture.

Achieve Exercise:

"It's kind of fun to do the impossible."
Walt Disney (1901-1966)

Chapter 7

NURTURING YOUR BODY AND LIVING WELL

Although this book is to encourage you to think bigger, differently and build greater aspirations for yourself, it's important that you understand the impact that your physical health has on your experience of life and the achievement of your goals.

What matters just as much as your mental approach is that you take care of your physical body *everyday* so that you can function as effectively as possible, be in good, strong physical health and protect yourself from possible future illness. A healthy body and a healthy mind are both essential to be your best self. What do you love doing that keeps you active and enjoying exercise?

Are you a team player- could you join a team activity? Do you like to train or exercise alone? Identify the 3 things that you enjoy the most and commit to doing them regularly – with some physical activity every day – even if that is a simple 30 minute walk.

Physical activity helps to create positive "feel

good" chemicals in the brain – and the more you experience the beneficial effects of exercise and activity the greater the positive balance in your life.

At the time of writing, we live in an age where the diets of many people are nutrient deficient and there is a lack of real understanding by the majority of the population as to how to eat a truly balanced diet. Most people don't know how good they can feel. We'd like to encourage you explore a range of different information that will help you to learn about essential nutrients and food groups which support your best body for life. Choose to reject the foods and products which are rich in sugar, salt and the wrong kind of fats. Simple, natural foods are best, and when you enjoy a varied, tasty nutritious diet, you'll discover an enhanced level of mental performance and sense of well-being which can be incredible to experience.

Extra reading for wholesome recipes and nutritional guidance. Here are some credible, reputable sources of further information which we encourage you to explore:

    Jamie Oliver

    Hugh Fearnley-Whittingstall

    Patrick Holford

    Gordon Ramsay

Eating healthily at all times and avoiding sugary,

salty, deep-fried and foods with bad fats is the way forward! Be nutritionally aware and discover foods that taste great and make you feel good too.

If you can successfully commit to achieve this for yourself, you will not only enhance your mental performance, but you will reduce your risk of lifestyle related illness and disease in the future, as well as helping to enhance your enjoyment of life in many other ways.

Always drink plenty of water to rehydrate and keep yourself in great physical condition all of the time.

SUMMARY

We've brought together a collection of proven ways to achieve success that have been around for centuries, but often only known to a small percentage of the population, as they may seem quite unusual to you. The power of your mind is the most truly incredible, untapped resource that you have.

It's true that much of what is written is very simple to understand as ideas and concepts – the challenge to you is to decide that you are worthy of being the very best version of yourself possible and then ACT and more importantly BELIEVE.

Developing self-discipline and a daily habit that will support your progress in life will lead you to a wonderfully fulfilling future.

It IS possible.

Your mind, your imagination and your thought patterns determine your actions, your self-image and your belief about what's possible.

YOU control them.

We hope that this introduction to a vast subject will encourage you to follow the guidance and read more from other authors in the future.

Abraham Lincoln once said

"The best way to predict your future is to create it".

"It's not what you say that defines you; it's what you do...."

Anon

Appendix:

Further Reading

The Secret	Rhonda Byrne
Think and Grow Rich	Napoleon Hill
Awakening the Giant Within	Anthony Robbins
Your Invisible Power	Genevieve Behrend

There are many more besides.

Enjoy and discover your true potential and fulfilment.

"What goes around comes around."

"Kindness is the language which the deaf can hear and the blind can see."

Mark Twain